Why Me, O Lord?

FINDING ANSWERS

Melissa Pennino Calegan

5 Fold Media
Visit us at www.5foldmedia.com

Why Me, O Lord?
Copyright © 2011 by Melissa Calegan

Published by 5 Fold Media, LLC
www.5foldmedia.com

Unless otherwise indicated, all Scripture quotations are taken from the Holy Bible, New Living Translation, copyright 1996, 2004. Used by permission of Tyndale House Publishers, Inc., Wheaton, Illinois 60189. All rights reserved.

ISBN: 978-1-936578-01-6

Dedication

This book is dedicated to everyone who has ever dealt with the unbearable pain of severe depression and the agonizing experience of despair, who, with God's help, can overcome.

May God Be Glorified!

Acknowledgements

Through this book, I want to give thanks to my Father in heaven, my Lord Jesus Christ, and the Holy Spirit for the countless miracles in my life. My prayer is that God is glorified through this work and even that lives may be saved.

I especially want to show my gratitude to my dear husband, Troy along with my boys, Tyler and Joshua; who, next to Jesus, are everything to me, and have given me the encouragement to complete this work.

I want to give honor to my pastors Mike and Elaine Millé. Without their teachings and leadership, I would not be the woman that I have become today. I am privileged to have them as my spiritual parents.

To my Dad, Grandmother, all of my family and friends that stood by me, and to my dear doctor: thanks for not giving up on me even when I gave up on myself.

To Frank and Shellie Garces, without your gentle nudging and allowing God to use you, this work would not be completed. I cannot express just how grateful I truly am. I pray that you are blessed in return.

Table of Contents

Introduction

She was dressed in a pair of old beat up black jeans and a long sleeved black shirt with an oversized dark green army jacket. Her hair was dark, long and straight. Her bangs hung down into her eyes. The only makeup that she wore was black eyeliner and a lot of it. She truly looked as if she wanted to be hidden from everyone. If she would have been able to crawl into a cave, she would have quickly vanished. The depression that she felt was so evident in her appearance. She wore it as though it was a heavy black quilt.

What caused this girl to be filled with so much darkness? Anyone could look upon her countenance and see complete despair. She was used and abused and it showed. Looking into her eyes seemed as though they were the eyes of someone with much more knowledge and experience than she should have had at her age. She was a child with the life experience of a woman. If anyone would happen to catch her eyes in a quick glance, they would immediately sense her agonizing pain. If people could only see past her anger; then they would see the heartache. She abhorred her life. The girl obviously wanted to die.

She tried to end it all. She took razors to herself. How many times did she cut her arms and wrists? How many suicide letters were written? No one knew. She used drugs to try to escape the pain. She drank alcohol every day after school—if she even went to school. She was in a living hell. She had no light in her or anywhere around her.

She was the type of girl that parents didn't want their sons to be near. Yes, she took a boy from a nice church-going family and before long innocence was gone from the both of them. He had a dark side too. He was the one who gave her the drugs that she had with her in school. This was the cause for her to get kicked out of the seventh grade. That's right, the seventh grade, she was only twelve.

"She" seems like a different person. "She" was me. That young, desperate, lost, lonely girl was really me. Yes, I was a different person. I had not yet met the man that would save my life… my Savior, Jesus.

This book is written as a true story about my life, in an attempt to inspire others. It is about circumstances that I have experienced throughout my life that has caused me to ask, "*Why me, O Lord?*" This work has taken me more than ten years to complete. At times it was just too painful for me so I would put it aside. I never had peace until the day that I completed writing this book. Through this I am answering a call from God on my life and hoping that someone may come to know the Lord Jesus Christ and His life changing mercy through this story.

Why Tell Your Story?

Why on earth would someone ever be proud and excited to tell people about all of the bad things in their past? I just didn't get it, until the Lord gave me a scripture. Revelation 12:11 "And they have defeated him by the blood of the Lamb and by their testimony…"

Sometimes I would think, *I don't want anyone to know the things that I have done or experienced in my life.* Then other days I'll think, *Why would anyone care about my past anyway? It wasn't that interesting.* It is different to other people. When someone meets you, they form an impression of you. To some people, that is who you are. They cannot imagine you any other way. Then, as you begin to tell your story, watch and see what happens. I often receive looks of shock and unbelief when I open up about my life. In Psalm 26:6-7 the Bible says, "I come to Your altar, O Lord, singing a song of thanksgiving and telling of all Your wonders." My story is life-changing. It is the past, and Jesus changed the direction of the path that I was on.

"No! Not you Melissa!" "I just can't believe that you would have ever done that!" and "You are not serious, are you?" and also, "That really happened to you?" are often the responses that I get from people when I begin to share my testimony. I get to explain to them that; yes, I did do those things and those things were done to me, BUT GOD… I've always loved those holy "buts!"

I. Desperation

Chapter 1
My Beginning

Chapter 1

My Beginning

My mother had three kids already by the time that she met my father. I have always admired him for not only taking on a wife, but also three boys including one with Downs Syndrome. They fell in love quickly. They were married only five months after they met, and he adopted all of the boys. Two years later they started trying for me.

I suppose my life started out very good considering that my parents had to try six months to get pregnant with me. I never could understand why some people, who don't even want children, easily get pregnant while other people who want children so desperately have such trouble conceiving. I want to say this before I go any further. No matter how you were conceived, it was God's plan for you. If you have heard that you were a mistake or an accident, or even worded so nicely to say that you were a great surprise; you weren't to God. His Word tells us in Psalm 139 that He knit me together in my mother's womb. He saw my unformed body. I am fearfully and wonderfully made. I have learned that He created me perfectly for my purpose. He created you perfect for your purpose too.

Although nothing can happen to us that God doesn't approve, I always hold on to the scripture in Romans chapter 8 that says that God causes everything to work together for the good of those who love God and are called according to His purpose for them. Growing up in my family home was very painful and scary. This was supposed to be a safe place for me, but it wasn't. I was abused by someone that was close to my family. It happened many times ever since I can remember until I was about ten. What good can possibly come out of that? Well, God has and will continue to show us! So keep reading.

One night my mom and dad were going out and I found out that I was going to be left alone with this person and that was when I decided that I wasn't going to take it anymore. So what if I was threatened with death? It wouldn't be so bad to die. If I was killed, then I would just go to heaven. What a good deal. Either way I would stop being hurt. As I saw it, no matter what ended up happening, I would be a winner.

I began to tell my mother everything that was happening. I told her very specific details that no ten-year-old child could imagine or make up. This moment impacted me forever. She told me that I was just dreaming it, that it couldn't be real. I was sobbing and desperately crying out to her. If she would not believe me, then she could not protect me. I insisted that this was real and I was not dreaming. She called my dad into the room and told him everything that I said. He wanted to take me to the hospital but she didn't want him to. They really didn't know what to do. Nobody knows what they would do in such a situation. So they finally confronted the person about it and, of course, he denied everything. Would he really admit that he was abusing me? I didn't know what to expect after I told. I didn't know if I would be killed or if it would happen again, only worse. Well he didn't kill me, but best of all was that he didn't hurt me again. It was over.

I should have told someone a long time before. I truly believed that I would be killed. Once I did try to stand up for myself. Imagine a little girl being victim to someone twice her size. I said "no!" He just laughed at me and started choking me. I remember the fear that I felt when I tried to breathe but couldn't. I really thought that I would die.

This person left town for a couple of years but unfortunately he was coming back. As soon as I found out about this, I started getting depressed and angry. I went to my mother for help. I told her that I was afraid that if he came back around that the abuse would start again. It was so hard for my mother to believe that it really happened to me. She really didn't want to believe it. She couldn't help me if she didn't think that it was true. How could I be protected?

So I did what any logical twelve-year-old girl who was afraid of being harmed again would do. I ran away. After being in the woods behind my house for a whole day and hearing my dad and my friends calling out for me, I gave up and went home. He was my hero! My dad didn't give up on me, and I was so relieved when he finally found me. I mean, who really wants to live in the woods anyway? I do remember when my dad walked me to the front door of our house, my mom met me at the door and she hugged me so tight that her fingernails were digging into my skin causing a lot of pain. I think back to what that hug meant to her. Now, all of these years later, I realize just how much that hug means to me.

At that point, they really tried to help me. My parents took me to a counselor for therapy. That was when I began my journey to learn to deal with the deep depression I had. *Why me, O Lord?*

Chapter 2
If God Loves Me So Much, Where Was He?

Chapter 2

If God Loves Me So Much, Where Was He?

This was the question that I had growing up. *Where was God when I was being abused? If He loves me, why did He let this happen to me?* I didn't do anything wrong. I wasn't a bad kid. I didn't deserve for this to happen to me! I didn't even ask to be born. If I had known this would happen, I wouldn't have wanted to be born. God is the One who made me, right? He is the One who could have done anything to stop this from happening, right? Where was He? Where were You, God? Why did You allow this horrible thing to happen to me?

How many girls (and even boys) have had these same questions that I had while growing up? Sexual abuse is so commonly discussed now. We hear of it so often. There used to be days that people didn't talk about these things. Thank God that we can talk about abuse now. The problem with keeping these issues a secret is that the victims feel ashamed and embarrassed. 1 Corinthians 6:18 says that sexual immorality is a sin against a person's own body. This is why people that have been sexually abused have even more guilty feelings than the perpetrator does. The abused feels as though she or he is responsible for this happening to them. They feel out of control of their own bodies. They are often confused and feel shame.

I remember crying and begging him to stop doing this to me. He told me that if I told anyone he would kill me. It is so confusing to a child that someone who is supposed to take care of her, love her, and protect her, is hurting her.

How can a child who is abused learn to trust anyone? In almost all cases of sexual abuse, the perpetrator is someone close to the family, or possibly even a family member. This is extremely hard on children. Kids are taught to obey adults and are expected to respect people in authority. However, when things like this happen they learn that they can't trust anyone. They may even begin to rebel against anyone in an authority position. I know this because that is exactly what I did.

People that are abused need to know that it is not their fault. They need the grace of God to help them to understand that they do not have to keep the secret. They do not have to accept the shame. It is not theirs to own. It is God's to take and heal.

Where was God? He was right there. He was by my side giving me the strength to endure what was happening to me. He loved me. He did not leave me. He did not forsake me. He suffered with me. God did not choose for this to happen to me. The person that abused me used his free will. He was influenced by satan. Just as I was by believing that God didn't care. He was demonically influenced and it was his choice.

There is even an example in the Bible of a girl that was raped by someone close to her. I remember the first time that I read that story. I was shocked! I was also a little relieved. I was not glad that this happened to her. But I was somewhat comforted knowing that someone else had been in my situation. God thought enough of Tamar and her situation to put the story in the Bible right there in 2 Samuel 13.

He put it there because He loves me so much and everyone else that was abused or raped. He turned my ashes into beauty. I was blessed because I had the opportunity to have years of counseling. And I had a doctor that went against the traditional therapy of having the abused re-live everything that happened. When I was in the hospital, one therapist wanted to use hypnosis on me because I didn't remember when the abuse started. My doctor said that if I didn't remember what happened, then that was a good thing. I didn't need to know. This is what my pastor calls "Holy Ghost amnesia," and I thank God for it!

People that have been abused work very hard to use their mind to exit their bodies as it is happening. Now I believe that when I did that, God was there holding me and comforting me. We often think that God is in control of all things and yes, ultimately, He is. But we must not forget, the whole point of God making us, was for us to have a free will to choose to love Him. Along with that free will includes the free will to make all of our own decisions.

It took many years for me to understand why a Holy God made a sinful man. He made us to have a free will because He wants us to follow Him. He wants us to make a choice to love Him. None of us would want to stay with a spouse that didn't love us. We may fool ourselves for a little while to try to avoid the pain of heartbreak, but ultimately, we would let someone we love go if that is what they chose to do.

Why Me, O Lord?

Could you imagine if we were all like a bunch of robots accepting commands from God? Love Me or die! How boring that would be. We would not have the unique features that make us who we are. God made us who we are in His own image. We are not His little robots; we are His children. As much as parents would want to have their children love them and do everything right, that just does not always happen.

This is why when bad things happen, we can't blame God. The tragedy of the twin towers in New York going down on September 11th is a perfect example. We cannot blame God for that. We must blame the people that flew the planes. All crimes are results of people making wrong decisions. That really has nothing to do with God, but God hurts from it too. It is His creation after all that are hurting each other. How would you feel if you had two kids and one of them hurt the other terribly? Imagine the anguish that you would feel inside. That is how God feels.

It's not a matter of where God was; it is a matter of who God is. He is my Deliverer, my Strength, my Comforter, and my Vindicator! One day He will show me how something good could come from something so terrible. He will give me an answer to my question: *Why me, O Lord?*

Chapter 3
Dressed in Black

Chapter 3

Dressed in Black

What is it about black? Women love to have that little black dress for all occasions because it helps us to look thinner and we blend in easily. We wouldn't be as noticed in a black dress as we would be in a hot pink dress. We tend to portray on the outside what is in the inside of us.

Black was my favorite color. To say that now seems so strange, but then it was very true. I wore black jeans, black tennis shoes, black shirts and almost always a black jacket. There was this one jacket that was even worse than wearing all of this black apparel. It was a green army jacket. I used a black marker and drew a cross in a circle on the back of it. I got that design from a few of my friends. All of us had a jacket like that. Once I put that thing on, it didn't come off.

I thought it would look cool to make my face look as white as I could, and my eyes as dark as I could. Can you imagine what I looked like? I was like death walking around in a thirteen-year-old girl's body. Parents, if your child is walking around looking like death, there is a reason. It is not just a phase. DO SOMETHING!

This was a warning sign to my parents that I needed help. They didn't catch it. In fact, one day I came home with my friend and I had been smoking marijuana, and my dad thought that I was on something but my mom said, "Oh, she is just happy that her friend is here." Come on folks; get real!

I did drastic things to get my parents to notice. Events like running away from home, attempting suicide, planning out how I would want my funeral to be... that is what it took to get their attention.

I didn't really want to be noticed. It was depression. I was tired of being so depressed all of the time. My life consisted of reluctantly going to school and coming home only to lock myself in my bedroom, turn off the lights, and lay on my bed. I would sob into my pillow and turn on my stereo as loud as I could stand it. It was not just any music. It was heavy metal music. Now I love a good beat and I am not against music. I just want you to know that it was music written about death. It was evil!

I would lay there in the dark blocking out the world and just cry until I fell asleep. Then I would wake up the next day and start all over again. At that time, I honestly couldn't tell you what was wrong with me.

I would do the same thing day after day. I hated school. I hated to wake up. I hated to do anything but sleep. I just didn't want to exist anymore. I couldn't explain why. *Why was I so depressed all of the time? What could I do about it? How could I change my life? Would it even be worth any effort?*

Now I know that the devil was trying to steal my life from me. As it says in John 10:10, The thief's purpose is to steal and kill and destroy. I have struggled with depression for most of my young life. I have been on and off of medications from as early as twelve. I often dealt with thoughts of suicide. There were times that I would try to cut my arms with razor blades. It was like I hated myself and I wanted to hurt. At the same time, there was some sort of control with that. At least if I did the cutting, I was in control of my pain. I did hurt myself in several ways.

I know that it was a real depression because it was an overwhelming sadness without a specific incident. I have had both types of depression; the kind that is circumstantial, and the kind that is not. The type that I am referring to here was definitely not circumstantial. I felt a real oppression. It was like a heavy blanket of darkness that had me trapped underneath it. It literally felt like something pushing down on me. I was in a hole that I just couldn't climb out of. The hole was no valley; it was a pit—a bottomless pit. There was no light at the top or at the end or near the bottom or anywhere. No peace could be found. It was black.

I guess that the school that I hated so much really helped me. When I did show up for school, I would spend a lot of time with the school counselors. I remember a time that I told one of them that I wouldn't see my sixteenth birthday. I actually promised that to her. Now I think back to how she must have felt hearing that from a child. What could she do? She only had so much power and influence in my life.

My threat to that school counselor almost came true when I was fourteen years old. I was taking an antidepressant daily and a refill had just been purchased. This particular night was not very different than any other night, except that I had a fight with my boyfriend.

Why Me, O Lord?

I just couldn't take it any more. I didn't want to live this life any longer. I had thought about it so many times. So on January 24th 1989, I took the whole bottle of the antidepressants. It is a bit ironic don't you think, for someone to attempt suicide with antidepressants?

I pause here with tears in my eyes and say to God, "Thank You for saving me from myself, Lord."

When my boyfriend called me back I told him what I did. Then he hung up on me and called on my parent's phone. Looking back, I really see God's hand here. My parents would almost never answer the phone. They usually just let the answering machine get the phone for them. But that night he called and kept calling until my dad did answer the phone. My boyfriend told him what I had done. He called the ambulance, and the paramedics were there in no time.

I remember them coming inside of the house and evaluating my situation. I was starting to feel the effects of the medicine that I had taken. My heart was pounding, my breaths were forced and my mind was becoming more and more stupefied with each minute that passed.

The medics were asking me questions that I really should have known such as my name and my phone number. I remember that I thought that I was saying everything correctly however; in the middle of speaking I realized that I was just rattling off a bunch of numbers. Then I began laughing so the medic asked me what was so funny and I told her that the numbers that I just said were not my phone number. I couldn't remember the phone number that I had my entire life. I also remember looking out of the window of the rear doors of the ambulance and thinking that we were going so fast.

The doctors were frantically trying to control me. There was such urgency in their actions. By this time I was completely out of control. I was fighting, kicking and screaming like a crazed maniac. At that time I may have weighed about 100 pounds and I was only 5'3" tall. I had to be restrained for them to insert the tube into my mouth to push down into my stomach. They had to pry my mouth open even after strapping my arms and legs down.

Once they were able to begin the pumping process, I remember thinking that it was amazing that I could actually see the food that I had for dinner that night, through the tube. After the pumping was complete, the doctors poured a black liquid into the tube. It came back up, all over the doctor and nurses. Due to the pumping, my stomach was unable to hold it down. The doctor started shouting at me that I had better hold it down or I would have to drink it. I tried my best to hold it down. I didn't want to drink it. After a little while had passed, a nurse came into my room with a cup of the black liquid. I had to drink it anyway. It was charcoal with water. It was used to neutralize the medicine that I took. It filtered out my intestines. A portable toilet was placed next to my bed. This is quite graphic and disgusting but I want people to know the truth. There is no reason to hide or sugarcoat anything. I would use any means possible to try to stop anyone from attempting suicide.

It was much later that I found out just how serious my condition actually was. I was in the hospital for about a week. The first three or four days I spent in the ICU. I had no clue that it took my body that long to become stable. The medicine that I took affected my heart, lungs and probably many other major organs. My wonderful grandmother, my dad's mom, had a word from God that I was in trouble; that death was after me. She didn't know what was going on because my parents didn't tell her. They didn't want her to be worried, but God told her to pray for me. She and her friends interceded for me and I believe that is what saved my life. I do still have to take medication today, over twenty years later, because of the damage that I caused to my liver. I really was very close to dying. But, I didn't die. I lived!

People that are considering taking their own life need to know what they are facing. It's not pretty. It is messy and selfish. It is real. It is death. It is eternal! Don't let the devil steal your life from you. I believe that when people are in a suicidal state of mind, they cannot comprehend the finality of the attempt. I know that I didn't. I couldn't see past the moment. I couldn't see the people that did love me. I cannot imagine what I put my parents through. Just the thought of a child, your own child, feeling that life is so bad that the only answer is to end it, is now too much for me to accept. At that time I couldn't think of another way out. All I knew was that I was in pain, and I wanted the pain to end. Would my darkness ever become light? Would this pain ever end? Would I ever get past this depression? *Why me, O Lord?*

Chapter 4
Help!

Chapter 4

Help!

My parents divorced when I was about fifteen years old. The day that my dad left, I thought that my world had ended. I was so devastated! I felt like he left me. I blamed myself, but it was not mine to own. Divorce is usually never about the children and it is never easy for anyone.

As time went on, my mother became depressed and it was hard for all of us to be there with all the changes. We got an apartment together. It was my boyfriend and I, along with my brother and his girlfriend. I was not even old enough to get a job. I only went to school five days for my entire freshman year of high school. I was in a bad situation.

It didn't last very long that way. I left and didn't go back home with my mother. My boyfriend and I went to his parent's home. My dad started to visit with me. I was still very cold toward him because of my hurt from him leaving. I had feelings of resentment and I was bitter. I felt abandoned and I was going to be mean to him to try to get back at him. That was so very wrong. My dad did the best that he could with me. I know that I put him through hell. He loved me so much that he couldn't let me keep going in the direction that my life was heading.

Why Me, O Lord?

I went to visit with him one weekend and he took me to church. I was really struggling to go in. I started crying in the parking lot and I was very confused. I was feeling very guilty and full of shame. I couldn't stop crying. One of my dad's friends began to speak to me. She told me that I was being touched by the Holy Spirit. We finally went inside and I cried through the entire church service. After church we went out to eat and my dad's friend was talking and I couldn't understand a word that she was saying because she had such a heavy Cajun accent. I was amazed that I could understand what she was explaining about the Holy Spirit and afterward she sounded totally different.

My dad waited for my boyfriend to have his 18th birthday, and then he came for a visit and told me that I had to pack my things and go with him. He lived an hour and a half away. Dad threatened to have my boyfriend arrested if I didn't go willingly because I was still a minor. I asked about my mom having legal custody and I was told that she gave it to my dad. So I went to live with him.

The apartment was horrible! Well, it was perfect for a single man that worked at night and had to sleep in the day, but not for a teenage girl that struggled with depression. It was just so dark. It was like a barn made of tin. The rain was so loud and it seemed scary to me. It had dark wood paneling and dark green shag carpet. Because my dad worked shift work, he put a covering on all of the windows to block out the light. Anyone that came would have to go through my bedroom to even get to the bathroom. I had no privacy at all. One morning as I was getting dressed for school, there was a mouse in the bathroom! I stood on top of the toilet for an hour waiting for my dad to come home from work, so that he could get rid of the thing. It was just not a very pleasant place.

I tried to keep a relationship with my boyfriend. My dad would let me go to visit my mother on the weekends and that is when I would see him. My boyfriend and I talked on the phone daily. My dad decided that I missed school too often, so he devised a plan. If I didn't go to school every day during the week, I was not allowed to go to visit my mother and my boyfriend. As time went on, I became more depressed. It got so bad that I actually told my dad that I thought that I needed to be put back on antidepressants. My dad didn't understand my cry for help. He didn't know what to do.

I had a pink marbled composition book that I used as a journal. I used that to get the attention that I so desperately needed. Inside the pages I had written out a plan for the type of funeral that I wanted. Details like what I wanted to be wearing, and the music that I wanted to be playing during the ceremony was also in there. I wrote in large bold print on the cover "PRIVATE" and left it on my bed when I went to school one day. That got his attention!

That day I was in gym class and my teacher informed me that I was being checked out of school. I said bye to my friend and told her that I would see her the next day. I had no idea just how wrong that statement would be. There was my dad, standing there on his crutches. He had a recent surgery on his foot and he still needed them to walk. I went up to him and didn't say a thing. He said to me to get in the car, so I did. We drove toward New Orleans, about a two hour drive, without saying a single word to each other. I thought that he was taking me to my mother's house. I figured that he had enough of me. After we passed the exit to her house, I thought that he was taking me to his mother's house. We passed that exit too. Now I was totally clueless. *Where were we going?*

Finally we pulled up at a hospital and we parked. Then I thought to myself, *oh this isn't about me and my journal at all; it's about his foot.* Then we walked into the hospital and I noticed that the security guards were watching me. As the doors closed they stood in front of them. I thought that it was a bit strange and I realized that this was about me. My dad had called ahead and the security was ready for me to run because my dad was on crutches. I was starting to get a little nervous. Then a man came out and escorted us into his office. My dad signed a few papers and then they explained to me what was happening. My dad admitted me to a hospital.

Okay, well maybe I could have gotten some help there except for one thing. This was the wrong place for me! It was supposed to be a branch of a psychiatric hospital that was closing down. It was actually the psych unit for a hospital in the city of New Orleans. It seemed more like a drug rehab than a psych unit. There were drug addicts there and they were all boys. They didn't really have a problem with depression like I did. This was definitely not the right place for me. Because I was the only girl, my room was next to the nurse's station so that they could watch me. After a few days I earned phone privileges. I called my dad and I begged him to get me out. The boys there were threatening to rape me that night. I was screaming on the phone with my dad and asking him if he could hear them yelling at me. He told me no, but he did hear. He came to get me that night. He lived two hours away but he got there as soon as he could.

I was so relieved and ready to just go home. I was so sorry that I had ever written in that journal. I was so stupid. I still had a very serious problem with depression that was very real. No matter where I was, depression was not just going to go away. The professionals knew that too. That is why they wouldn't let my dad just take me home. The only way that he could leave that hospital with me was to transfer me to another one. That is exactly what he did. I went to a private psychiatric hospital.

This place was like paradise compared to the other hospital. There were people there with the same issues that I had. They were the same age as me. We became like a family to each other. We all fit together. The counselors there were great too. They really seemed to care about the patients. They took their time with us. We had group sessions as well as individual times of counseling. Things were looking up for me.

I had two things on my side; a great doctor and very good insurance. At the time, I didn't think these things were so great. Most patients would come and go anywhere from three days to three weeks. Well, three days, three weeks, and even three months came and went for me and I was still there. I was making progress but I was not about to leave any time soon. After a while, I was getting tired of following all of the rules. I was getting tired of everyone else leaving me there. I started to get angry with the staff, my doctor and my parents. No one would help me to get out. I was really getting tired of being there, but I still wasn't leaving anytime soon.

I had many counseling sessions with my parents. We were able to work through the hurt, rejection and trust issues that I had toward my dad and my mom. We did these sessions together and individually. Today I thank God for all of these things. Without all of the counseling, I would never have been able to get over the things in my life.

Why Me, O Lord?

I recognized my need for God even when I was there in the hospital. I didn't know the first thing about having a relationship with Him, but I knew that I needed Him. I had a Bible and I tried to read it, but I didn't understand anything in it. I was trying to read the Bible as though it was any other book. I was starting in the beginning and trying to read the names and I just could not understand anything. This one begot that one, but I didn't even know what *begot* meant. I was so lost when it came to the concepts of God.

As time went on, I became more and more desperate to get out. I was trapped; or at least I felt that way. Why did I get stuck with the good insurance and the good doctor? Why couldn't I just be like everybody else that gets to go home after a few days or weeks? Why do I have to stay here this long? *Why me, O Lord?*

I thought that I was over the depression, but I was wrong. I was trying to get one over on everyone but it was just an act. It was just like when I overdosed and told that doctor that evaluated me that I was fine. The difference was that this time, my doctor cared, and I hated him for it.

By the time that I really was ready to go, my doctor refused to release me until my dad got a brighter and happier place for us to live. I described the conditions of our apartment to him and he would absolutely not let me go back there. I was very glad that my doctor made my dad get us a better place. I think that my dad was too.

I was there for a total of seven months. That's right, seven months! I'm not sure but I'll bet that I am on the list of top ten people that have ever stayed there that long. It was a very hard road, but it was well worth it. I have to say that all of the wonderful counseling would be nothing without God's touch on it. I have no idea if my doctor was a Christian or not. This I do know… God did it. God used my doctor and counseling to change my life.

My doctor said to my dad, "I was given a mess, but I give back to you, a ballerina princess." If I would have left after three weeks or even three months, I would not have gotten all of the benefits that I needed. I left, after seven long months, but then it was with a good relationship with both of my parents. While I was there, I actually learned to smile. That was worth it all!

It was time to return to the real world. While I was in the hospital, I was approached by one of my teachers with the idea of getting my GED while I was there. She told me that I would pass the test easily enough and I wouldn't have to go back to school when I got out. I thought about it and I decided against it because I was looking at a new life. I thought that going to high school would be a good experience for me and I really didn't know what else I could do. So I didn't take the test.

Looking back, I wish that I would have done it. High school was not good. At least it was not for me. I was not one of the pretty girls. I was not a cheerleader. I was not even athletic. I was now two years older than everyone else in my class. That is because I was kicked out of the seventh grade for possession of marijuana, so I repeated that grade. Then I blew another year of my life by only going to class five days of my first year of ninth grade and it took me two weeks to do that. I didn't fit in anywhere with anyone.

Outside of school I managed to have a friend and a boyfriend. I dated the guy for a couple of years and we were very serious and talking about marriage. There was a problem though. As I got to know him and his family better, I realized that they were a very close family. I was the complete opposite of that and it was hard for me to understand such closeness. So when his grandfather offered to put a trailer home in the rear yard for us to live in after we marry, I sort of freaked out at the idea of living in the in-laws backyard. We broke up. Even though I didn't want to marry him, I had a hard time after our breakup. I became very lonely.

Looking back, I see that I was searching for a man to help me feel complete. At that time my goals in life were to get married, have a bunch of kids and maybe be lucky enough to own a home. The Lord had different plans for me, but I couldn't yet see them.

I went through the motions of high school with not many friends. I didn't really go to football games or any dances. I don't think that anyone noticed me at all. Many days I would be "sick" and have to stay home from school. When I did decide to go, I would take a few shots of my dad's whiskey before leaving home. My senior year was better because I had a great schedule. I only had to go in for three classes a day. I got out at 10:30 a.m. and I was driving, so I decided to get a job.

I got a job as a cashier for a grocery store. I noticed something about myself. I took on responsibility well. All of those years of skipping school, anyone would think that I would call into work "sick" but, I never did. In fact, I was so dedicated to my job that my dad came in to talk to my boss when we had to evacuate for a hurricane, because I wanted to work and I didn't want to leave. The only reason that I left that job is because it was time to go to college.

I actually did it! I was twenty years old at the time, but I did graduate, on stage with my graduating class. Quite a few of the girls happened to be single pregnant teenagers. I remember thinking to myself, *don't they know what causes that and how to avoid it?* Be careful judging people. You never know someone's circumstances and you never know when you will be ruled by the same judgment.

During this time, my dad was faced with a difficult decision. He had to either lose his job or move to another part of the state to keep his employment. I was almost finished with high school and I was doing very well with my job. He didn't want to move me, but he had to go. It was decided that I would move in with my friend. She was a few years older than I was and she was already on her own. It was a good way for her to help me and my dad gave her some money for my living expenses. It was only for a few months.

I started college while I was living there and I was commuting an hour everyday for 7:30 a.m. classes. That soon became tiresome and I asked my dad about putting me in an apartment near school. I moved and was only minutes from school and my dad was supporting me. It should have been great. It didn't feel great. I was very lonely while I was there. I didn't really know how to study because I never had to in high school. I didn't know that I would have an opportunity to go to college; so I didn't really plan for it with my choices of classes in high school. I was not prepared for what college had in store for me.

I stayed in that apartment for six months. Just before it was time to renew my lease, my dad admitted to me that it was a financial strain to him for me to be in the apartment and not working to help with rent or spending money. He told me to either get a job or go to a cheaper school. So I did both.

I talked to my mom about moving in with her and going to the local community college. I would finish my semester at the university that I was already going to. I would just have to commute there for a while. She thought it wouldn't be a problem. We didn't know what we were getting into.

Chapter 5
Consequences

Chapter 5

Consequences

My mom and I forgot to consider how my moving in with her would affect our relationship. Things were different now. She was remarried and I was an adult. It's hard to go back home and we didn't really get along as well as we should have at that point. She was concerned about me being in school and working.

I got a job working in a daiquiri shop. I was a bartender. I was very shy and didn't have a high self esteem at all. With a job like this I was forced to talk to people. It was good for me in a way, because it helped me to learn how to initiate conversations with people.

It was my second day working at the daiquiri shop when I met a man that I began dating within a few days. Everything was great in the beginning until I developed a problem. If I wasn't working, I was sitting with him on the other side of the bar. We were always there. It was like a party all the time, a party that involved me getting drunk every night.

After he and I were dating for about three months, I started having problems with my mom. She was concerned about my drinking and about my education. We had a huge fight and I was asked to leave the house.

I then got an apartment with my boyfriend. I was in school during the day and working at the daiquiri shop at night. While I was working, he was there with me. It wasn't long until I got pregnant and was not married.

I was so scared to tell him. I thought that he would be mad, but he wasn't. He was actually happy. What a relief I felt. The only problem was when I began to work at a different location because my boyfriend didn't like the other location. That was when I realized that he was there every night, not because of me, but because he wanted to be there with his friends. I felt like he didn't want to spend any time at all with me. I felt alone.

I had unfairly placed expectations upon him that we never agreed to. He was just being himself and I am not trying to say that he was bad. He wasn't. He just didn't meet my fantasy of what my life was supposed to be like. I was not living the perfect "fall in love, get married, have a baby" life that I had dreamed of.

We broke up. He decided to stay in the same apartment with me until after the baby was born so that he could take care of me and the baby.

There I was, pregnant and not married. *How could this happen to me? This happened to girls that were too stupid to use birth control,* I always thought. *This happened to other people, not me. How could I be pregnant from someone that didn't love me the way that I desired to be loved? Why me, O Lord?*

Once the baby came I was very embarrassed about being a single mother. God had to bring me to my knees about the whole issue. I was so judgmental toward others in years past. Now that same situation came upon me.

My life wasn't at all what I thought it would be. We were not happy together. I didn't want to be that way anymore. I didn't want my baby to grow up in that lifestyle. I started looking for a full-time job. We agreed that he would stay until I got another job and he got an apartment.

God provided for me and my baby. It was a starting position at a chiropractor's office. I went to work and he got another apartment so we were now free to separate, and we did. No matter how much I loved my baby, I was so ashamed to be a single mother.

It's not often when you live a life of sin that you can thank God for the consequences of it. I was very fortunate that I responded to the result of my sin the way that I did. I became a very responsible mother. I wanted a better life for my baby than the one that I was living when I first had him. My son's father was not my fantasy but he is a good dad. He has taken care of our child. What I went through was very difficult, but because I received my son through it, I would never choose to not have gone through it all. Because I have my son, I rejoice. I thank God for giving me my son, Tyler.

II. New Life

Chapter 6

The New Life

Chapter 6

The New Life

After I had my baby, I quit drinking and I worked very hard to save money for a down payment on a house. I bought a four bedroom and two bathroom home. It was quite an accomplishment for a young, single mother to do. It was the goodness of God. He was providing for me.

One day I was visiting my mother and an old friend felt strongly to pass by my mother's house. We were friends from the seventh grade. Circumstances of life had temporally disconnected us. She knew that I didn't live there anymore. She didn't even know where I lived. But thank God, she followed the leading to pass by. I just happened to be there. We talked and caught up and became as close as ever.

One night I was on the phone with her and I was crying about how lonely I was. She mentioned a single's group at her church. I thought this is the kind of place that I could meet a great guy. So I told her that I would go check out her church sometime. It took a few weeks for me to get there, but I had a praying grandmother. She and her friends prayed for me and never gave up. Those were the seeds that were planted and my friend came along and watered them.

Then one day, I finally made it. I had to really push to make myself go and I didn't have the proper clothes. I went anyway. I was wearing cut-off shorts and a sleeveless shirt. I sat in the back and someone came to me. She was so nice. She could tell that it was my first time there and I was so nervous. She invited me to sit in the front of the church with her and I agreed. Then she brought me right up there. She was in the second row! Then the music started. It was exciting and modern. I thought, *What is this? I've never heard this kind of music in church before.* The people seemed to be having fun, a lot of fun. I was just standing there looking around and wondering what I should do. I had no idea what to expect at White Dove.

Well, I started clapping. And I loosened up. I really enjoyed the worship. Then it was time for the message to be delivered. There was the preacher. The words that came from his mouth went directly into my heart. They were medicine to my wounds. He was not like any other preacher that I have seen before. This was not like any church that I had been to before. What kind of church is this? This is wild!

I found my friend after service was over. She was so glad that I made it. So many times I tried to go, but something always came up. I told her several times that I would be there, only to disappoint her. It's good that she never stopped inviting me. After my first time attending, I couldn't stay away from that place. I was hooked. Then I noticed that I wasn't even looking for a man, but I was learning about Jesus and not just learning about Him, but having a relationship with Him.

When I got saved I learned that I could have a new life. God didn't care about the life of sin that I lived before.

That is why it is called being "born again." I became a new person. I was free from my guilt and shame. I was made new and I was redeemed. I discovered joy. For the first time in my life I had joy; joy and peace. I was free from darkness!

Shortly after I got saved, the Lord gave me a new job. I worked with all Christians. After I was at the church for about four months, I saw someone that I knew in the choir. That was the first time that I had seen the choir. I would always go to the earlier service that didn't have the choir sing. I went to her to tell her that I enjoyed hearing the choir and asked if people were required to sing good to be in it. She told me that the Lord said to make a joyful noise; He didn't say that it had to be good. The next thing I knew, I was in the choir. That was really incredible because I can't sing! They didn't care. They loved me. I finally fit in somewhere.

I thought that I started going to church to find a nice boyfriend. But I found so much more. I found Jesus! Well, He found me. I found a new life that I didn't know existed. I found eternal life. I found friends who became a family to me. I found love and acceptance for myself. I found healing from the past. I found a purpose for my life. I began to see goodness come from the bad things in my life. I didn't even go to a single's event until I was there for about six months.

It was about that time that I went to the church in the middle of the day crying my eyes out. I had to talk to someone. I was begging for counseling because I was so depressed. I just couldn't understand why God hadn't given me a husband yet. I was in church for six months already. I had been praying for so long! The minister that I spoke with told me to seek first the kingdom of God and to wait on the Lord.

Why Me, O Lord?

Being in the choir and working with Christians really helped me to grow and to be strong in my Christian walk. But beware! The devil will always try to trap you. He tried with me.

One day a man that I knew from my past walked in the office. This was a man who I really wanted to be with, but he moved to another state before our relationship could grow. He went to my previous job and asked about me. They told him where he could find me, and he did! When I walked up to him I turned so red and was dripping with sweat. I was so nervous. I said to him that "I go to church now." "I am saved." That was all that I could say, and I said it to him over and over again! I don't know if I was trying to convince him or myself. Then after a few minutes, he left. I haven't seen him again since.

Yes! I passed that test. Unfortunately that was not the only time that the devil would try to tempt me. Years passed and I was still crying and praying for a husband. Someone taught me to pray specific things to God. So I made a list of everything that I thought that I wanted in a husband. I wrote down things like a beautiful smile, broad shoulders, tanned skin, beautiful eyes, and so on.

The devil heard my prayer and he answered it. When God's answer was for me to wait, the devil stepped in to give me his counterfeit. This time, I didn't pass the test. I forced this relationship. It never should have happened. I met him where I was working at during that time. I thought that he was so perfect for me. He was not. I didn't pay attention to the first "red flag" that came my way. I was the one who invited him to church. He was not even a Christian. He talked about wanting to marry me and buy me a dream house.

My mom told me that he just sounded too good to be true. She also warned me that he probably was not true. He got me to start drinking again. One night he cooked dinner for me and I still believe that something was in my drink because I blacked out. The next thing that I knew it was too late.

The next morning, when I woke up, I realized what had happened and I said to him that we had to get married very soon. Just two days later we were in church and my pastor stopped right in front of the section that I was in. I'll never forget the way that he spoke with such authority as he held his head down looking toward the floor. He had a word from God. He said "Sweetheart, that man that you want to marry is not sent to you by God, but he is sent to you by satan, to pull you away from God." I knew that he was talking about me, but I didn't want to admit it. My friend asked me if I was alright. I told her that I was fine and that the word was not for me. I lied to her. It was for me. I was not fine. My heart was beating hard and I felt sick to my stomach. I also felt very faint. God spoke directly to me through my pastor.

I didn't listen to the warning. I figured that it wasn't that bad to continue in sin. We already did, and now we had plans to marry. Then I got a call from my friend. She said that she had to tell me something even if it meant that she would risk our friendship. I asked her to tell me what it was, and she said that she was praying for me and she knows that this man was sent to me by the devil and not by God. I didn't want to listen to her either. I wanted more than anything to be married. I just couldn't go through the pain of being lonely again.

A few weeks later, God had enough of me not taking the warnings that He was sending. Something had to happen.

It did. My boyfriend told me that he had just found out that his ex-girlfriend was pregnant with his baby. He said that she was on drugs and that he had to go to be with her to make sure that she didn't do anything that would harm the baby. He was leaving town in a few days to go to be with a woman that he didn't love. He said that he loved me and that this was breaking his heart. He knew that I would understand that he had to take care of his unborn baby. I said goodbye to him.

About three days passed and I hadn't eaten anything. I couldn't understand what had happened. You see, I wanted so badly to believe that God had sent this man to me, that I did. I believed a lie. I questioned God. *Why did You give this man to me only to take him away from me? Why did You allow us to be together and fall in love, if You knew that You had already created a baby? Why did You create the baby? Why did this happen to me? Why me, O Lord?*

I blamed God. All too often people do what they want to do and when it doesn't turn out the way that they want, they blame God. The Lord was good to me. He answered my questions that day. I went home during my lunch time and I was crying and praying. I asked God all of those questions. He told me to call my boyfriend. I thought that the idea was crazy because he had left town three days ago. God impressed so much on my heart to just call, so I did. I finally obeyed God.

When I called I was expecting the phone to be disconnected, but it wasn't. Someone answered. It was her. I was shocked! I asked to speak to him and she said that he was not there. She asked who I was. I told her that I was his girlfriend and she asked me if he told me about her. I told her everything that he told me about her. I told her what he said about the baby and the drugs. She told me what I had just realized in my heart. He lied about everything. She was his girlfriend before I had ever come along and she was never, not his girlfriend. She was not on drugs and she was never pregnant. He actually cheated on her with me!

She told me that he would be there in a few minutes and he walked in while the two of us were on the phone. He asked her who she was talking to and she told him that it was me, so he quickly hung up the phone. I decided that I would take a ride over to his apartment before I went back to work. When I got there, she answered the door and I told her that I just wanted to say something to him. I think that she wanted me to tell him off, so she got him to come to the door. She told him to face me and take what he deserves. As he stood there in front of me, I was trembling. I was so hurt and angry. I looked him in the eyes and I calmly spoke to him. I said, "I forgive you, but you need to face God about what you did to me and pray that He has mercy on you." I also said, "You knew that I wanted to wait until I was married before having sex again and you took that away from me, God will deal with you." Then I turned around and walked away.

I believe that I was a greater witness for Christ by the way that I handled that situation instead of yelling and screaming like a maniac. It was only by God's grace on me that I was speaking calmly to him. It was God's grace that made me call that day. It was God's grace that stopped the whole relationship before it went any further.

Now my new life returned to all of the hurt and disappointment that I had before. I was alone again.

Chapter 7

All Things Work Together

Chapter 7

All Things Work Together

Remember back when I said what good could possibly come from that horrible experience of abuse? This brings me to a few years later, after I was a single mother and a Christian; God showed me how it could possibly be a good thing that I went through abuse. A twelve-year-old girl came to me for help. She told me that the same person that abused me told her what he had done. She asked me if it was true. I told her that it was true and I asked why he told her. Her response was "Because he did it to me too!" She was raped and abused.

There I was; a twenty-four-year-old woman in charge of a three-year-old son, a full time job, a house, being a helper to my mother and now I was the only person able to help this twelve-year-old girl who was raped. Her parents didn't help her. I had to take care of this. God and my wonderful church helped me! I called my church and asked them what I should do and they sent us to a psychiatrist. The doctor had to call the authorities to report the issue.

She lived with me for six months. I took her to church and she got saved! I hate to think of the things that could have happened to her if I had not gone through what I went through. The girl could have ended up dead if she wasn't able to tell me what he did to her. She wouldn't have told me, if he didn't tell her that he abused me also. Because of this, I was able to thank God that I was once abused.

Through it all I learned that God was there. Yes, this person's free will was a great factor in this part of my life, however, God ultimately allowed me to go through all of this for a greater good. I think of the butterfly struggling to make its way out of the cocoon. If someone was to help by making a hole in it, then it would never develop the strength that is necessary for it to fly and it would only die. God has allowed me to have my struggles and I am a stronger woman because of it and I do thank God for it.

I'm not at all trying to say that God wanted any of this to happen. No way! I'm trying to explain that God will take a horrible situation and make something wonderful come out of it. If we get out of His way and allow Him to do His will, we will find that no matter how much something hurts, how agonizing or how bad a situation can be, God will ultimately take it and create something so wonderful out of it. We have to trust Him. He is the Artist and we are His canvas.

Chapter 8
Mom

Chapter 8

Mom

My son, Tyler, was born at the end of June and by the beginning of August my mom was diagnosed with cancer. She lost her voice a few months before that. The doctors kept telling her that she had laryngitis. Finally she went to another doctor who was very good and took time with her. She felt my mom's neck and noticed a lump. She ordered tests.

The results showed that she had inoperable lung cancer that spread to her lymph nodes. The Oncologist told her that with no chemo-therapy she might have six months to a year to live. He ordered treatment immediately. Mom stopped working and was put on disability. She looked at the bright side. At least she didn't have to work anymore.

I moved in with my mom before I bought my house. That helped me to save my money and I helped her while I was there. Though we had many hard years, this turned out to be a very good time for us. I am not exactly sure if it was the cancer or the birth of my son, but God worked through both situations and we became very close.

Tyler and I lived with my mom for about a year. I worked very hard to save money to buy my house. When I finally did buy the house, everyone was proud of me; especially my mom. Maybe she was just glad to get me out of her house.

Just kidding, I know that she really was proud of me. I had accomplished something pretty good. The odds were against me. I am not sure of the exact numbers but, I'll bet that not many twenty-three-year-old single moms are in a position to buy their own home. Now I know that it was God's provision that helped me to do that.

At that time I was still a baby Christian. As most new believers, I believed everything that the Bible said. So, of course I believed that God would heal my mom. I believed with all of my heart that He would. I would teach my mom things that I would learn in church or by just reading my Bible. We would have lots of conversations about life and death.

She did fairly well with the chemo treatments. It worked for a little while. But then the cancer came back, and the doctors would start the treatment again. This went on for about three years. She came to visit me one day right after a doctor's appointment and I noticed that she was blinking her eyes and moving them around a lot. When I asked her what was wrong, she pulled me to the side and told me that as she was leaving the doctor, she felt a pop behind her eye and then she had a blind spot. She couldn't see out of a part of her eye.

I got upset with her for not turning around and going back to tell the doctor. She didn't even tell her husband! So, I caused a big commotion and made her go back to the doctor. After running more tests, they found six tumors in her brain. Radiation treatment began right away. She wore a patch over the eye with the blind spot. The other eye was still working fine.

She had me call my brother, Jerry, to tell him the news. I didn't understand why she wanted me to do it, but I did what she wanted. He asked me if I thought that he should come at that time to visit with her. He was already scheduled to come a few weeks later. I believed with all my might that God was going to heal her. I told him that I didn't think that he had to come. He could just wait for the visit that he had planned.

Then about two weeks later my mom was watching my son for me and when I got back to her house she told me that she would not be able to watch him anymore. I got very angry with her because she said that she didn't want to be watching him when she dies. I started yelling at her saying that she didn't want God to heal her. She told me that if God was going to heal her, He would have done it by this time. In my eyes, she was giving up. She even told me that she wanted me to have a meeting with my pastor for counseling because I was in denial. I couldn't believe what I was hearing. *She said that to me?* I left the house angry and thinking that she was the one that had a problem with denial, not me!

Later that evening she called me because she was so excited! She felt something pop behind her eye again, but this time it helped her. The blind spot was gone! She could see fine. She said that she even felt great. She wanted me to pick her up the next day to take her shopping. I was so happy and I told her yes, I would be glad to take her shopping right after church. For some strange reason she wanted to know what time I would be there. I told her that I would be there right after church but she insisted that she wanted to know what time. So, I told her that I would be there at 1:00 p.m.

The next morning I woke up happy and excited about my mom feeling well and I went off to church. Worship was so amazing that day. In fact, the Holy Spirit took over the service and my pastor didn't even get a chance to preach. That is how powerful that worship service was. I came out of the choir stand and there I laid over the steps to the altar. I was in deep prayer thanking God for making my mom better. Then the

Why Me, O Lord?

Lord spoke to my heart and said, "I will heal your mother, but not the way that you want Me to." I knew in an instant that she was about to die. I thanked the Lord anyway as I sobbed.

Well church did let out earlier than I expected because Pastor wasn't able to preach that day. It was earlier than my mom expected me so when a friend asked me to go have lunch, I decided to go. I remember passing my mom's neighborhood and having a strange feeling. One that I don't have words to describe. But, I just shook it off and went to eat.

I left the restaurant about 10 minutes after 1:00 p.m. As, I turned to go down the street of my mom's house, I saw an ambulance and a couple of cop cars. I stopped my truck in the middle of the street, grabbed my son and ran to the house with him in my arms. The police stopped me before I could reach the door. I said that this was my mom's house and they refused to allow me to go inside. I asked them to tell me what was going on, and the man just told me to wait there and he went in.

My mom's husband came out. The cop went to tell him that I was outside. When he saw me he just broke down into tears. He said that she was gone. My response was, "what do you mean she is gone, I came to get her." I knew what he meant, but how could it be? She was feeling better. She wanted me to take her out shopping. I just couldn't believe it. My mom was dead. Her body lay lifeless in the house and I couldn't go in to see her. They would not let me.

She always said that she did not want to have a death bed. She didn't want people to be next to her and crying and holding her hand. She wanted to be alone. Well, she was alone when she died. That morning, she told her husband that she was so tired and she would not be able to go with me. She said that she needed some things from the store so she sent him. He wanted to wait for me to get there to be with her, but she insisted that he go. He left the house at about 12:30 p.m. He got home at 1:00 p.m. and she was dead. The paramedics told me that it was a sudden thing for her. Well, she got what she wanted. She died alone. I was blessed that I was able to tell her many things that she had to look forward to when she would die.

One thing about having a disease and knowing that you are about to die is that you can make sure to have the conversations that you want to have. My mom and I had many of those conversations. I would often read from the bible and describe Heaven to her. I gave her hope in what to look forward to. She found much comfort in that.

One of my favorite conversations was when she told me that the one thing that she felt as though she would miss would be my wedding. She wished that she would see me get married. Not because she was worried about me, because I was a very independent woman. I took good care of myself and my son. She just wanted to see me happy. She knew the heartache that I had in being alone. I joked with her saying that I could go to buy a dress and take pictures with her. But she said that we couldn't do that because it would be cheating. She would never know just how much I wished that we would have done that.

I see other ladies my age at the shopping mall walking with their mothers and pushing a baby in a stroller or sitting together in church. Sometimes I do get a little grieved. That time is so precious, and it is never long enough. No matter how much time you have with a loved one, it is never enough time. And it is always a shock. If the person is sick or not, it will surprise you when they die. We knew for three years that my mom was sick. We knew that she was facing death. But it was still very much a surprise to me when she died.

My brother didn't get to see her. It was my fault. I told him not to come. *Why was this burden on me? Why did my mom make me call him? Why did he ask me if he should come? Why was it my fault that my brother didn't get to say goodbye to our mom?* I honestly didn't think that he had to change his plans. Why would he? God was going to heal her. I'm so sorry to my brother for that.

My grandparents and my aunt and uncle were there for me. This was my dad's family and they were the people that stepped up to help me with the issues that came with losing my mother. Without the grace of God and the love and comfort from my family and also my friends at church, I couldn't have made it through.

I miss my mother. I think that she just accepted that she would die. I believe that she may have even been a bit relieved. She had lived a rough life. But when it was all over, she still got what she wanted. God showed mercy to her and He gave her what she wanted. She was alone.

Why God? Why did she have to die so young? Why didn't she have faith to be healed? She didn't want to be healed! Was my faith in vain? What about having the faith of a mustard seed? I had much more. Well, I know that she was truly healed. Why couldn't she just live long enough to see my wedding day? She didn't even get to meet my husband. That was her only regret that she told me about. Maybe she saw it from heaven? Why did the last time I see her end with an argument? Was she right? Was I really the one with the problem of denial? Why me, O Lord?

Chapter 9
Learn To Enjoy the Wait

Chapter 9

Learn To Enjoy the Wait

The hardest thing about waiting for the perfect spouse is, well, the waiting. We feel lonely and incomplete. I know when I was still single, I was constantly crying out to God. Where is he Lord? I am talking about not just crying out but really screaming out to God.

You know that feeling that you get deep in the pit of your gut that just aches to be filled. There is no way to ease the pain. We go through feelings of inadequacy. We have questions for God, such as, *What is wrong with me? Am I not pretty enough? Am I not nice enough? Am I not smart enough?* (Maybe I'm too smart!) *What did I do to deserve this? What did I do that makes me so bad that no one wants to be with me? Why do I have to be alone while I watch all the people around me getting what they want? It seems that so many people take what they have for granted. They show no respect for their mate. Is it too much to ask for? I just want to be in love and have a husband who loves me. Why do I have to be single, God? Why me, O Lord?*

Everyone that I knew was familiar with my strong desire for a husband. One lady told me about Proverbs 18:22 which states "The man who finds a wife finds a treasure, and he receives favor from the Lord." It took me a while to get exactly her reason for telling me this verse. It wasn't what I thought at first. It was *he who finds a wife* that was the key point that she was trying to get across to me. He must find her. It shouldn't be her searching for him.

Ladies, we must wait on God to lead the right man to us. I have met people who have told me that they know that they married someone who would not have been God's choice for them. These people feel stuck with their spouses. Yes, some love each other and they have kids and are blessed. However, they will not reap the full blessing of the Lord. They will not have all of the wonderful benefits of a godly marriage. They are not in God's perfect will for their lives. How much happier could they have been in life if they would have waited for the spouse that God had chosen for them?

Men, I urge you, please seek God's will before you ask someone out, or even spend time with a girl. You don't want to lead people on. In fact, you yourself may be the one lead on and may miss out on God's will. SEEK GOD FIRST!

Young singles, keep this in mind. If you have any thoughts of not telling your parents about a relationship that you are in or are considering becoming involved in, THERE MAY BE SOMETHING WRONG HERE! Okay I know that not all cases are the same. But, in most cases, if you feel like you want to hide something about a relationship, then that should be a red flag screaming at you. STOP! Don't do it.

Our Father in heaven knows what is best for us. I thank God for not allowing me to get married to some of the men that I thought, *He could be the one.* I don't want to think about the kind of lifestyles that I may have had. I'm talking about church people too. Some church folks are crazy!

We know that we all have been wild at some point, and it seems that we are all looking for someone to rescue us from the craziness. We must seek the Lord to rescue us, not a spouse. None of those men would have been good for me.

God knows just who fits you. He had it planned out long before you ever thought of wanting someone in your life. He created your perfect mate especially for you. Wait on Him. He will lead you down the right path. He will give you what you need when you need it.

God is our Parent. He is our Father. He wants to give us good things but for our safety and well being, He must make sure that we are ready to receive it. There is really nothing that you can do to make yourself ready. We must learn to seek the Lord.

Remember that God knows your motive. Even if you don't want to admit that your true motive for doing something is to receive the blessing of a spouse. I have tried everything that I could think of. I claimed scriptures. I spoke God's Word back to Him. I prayed and prayed without ceasing. I begged God. I pleaded with Him. I even tried to bargain with Him. People were always telling me that God will send him when I stop looking. I tried to stop looking. In all of these instances, my motive was to get my blessing. God knew that it just wasn't my time.

Sometimes I would think that I had it all together so it must be my future husband that was holding things up. He must be the one that God is working on because I was REALLY READY! I would even get a little mad at him (my future spouse) for holding things up. I didn't even know the man or anything about him and I was angry with him already. I know it sounds really bad. It was really bad. Thank God that He gave me good friends. Everyone was so patient with me. As I am writing this, I am thinking that I probably couldn't stand it if I had a friend like me.

Loneliness is a very hard feeling to get through. There were many times that I thought that I just couldn't take it anymore. I knew that God was the one who was ultimately in control. He could give my husband to me at any time. But He would not do it. "Why God?" I would cry out. Did He hear me? Did He know how painful it was for me to be alone? Did He even care? Yes! He heard me. He knew my pain, and yes, He cared very much.

We really must be careful of how we handle these things. I could have had my blessing so much sooner than I did but it was my fault. It was a case of self sabotage. I was at a wedding for some friends in our singles group. I was so happy for them, but you wouldn't think so if you looked at me. The countenance on my face was the complete opposite. Another friend asked me what was wrong and I burst into tears. She took me to another room and prayed with me. As happy as I truly was for my friends, I was just as sad for myself. I was lonelier than ever before. I slipped out the door behind some other guests as they were leaving. I went home and cried.

I found out years later that my husband could have become my boyfriend on that day. He wanted to talk to me so desperately. The reason that he didn't was because he saw the sadness upon my face. He was just about to talk to me as I was walking to the door to leave. The very one that I was grieving for was right there and wanted to be with me but my own self focus prevented that from taking place.

I prayed and I cried over and over again. I waited and months passed. Then years passed. I kept praying and waiting. One day when I was praying, the Lord impressed upon my heart that I have already met my husband. I looked around the church. I saw a few men that I knew but thought that maybe I missed God. You know that story in 1 Samuel 16, when Samuel went to anoint David as king and Jessie brought in his big and strong sons. Samuel knew that it was none of those men and asked Jessie if he had another son. Jessie told him yes but he was a small and young boy. Samuel explained that God didn't look at men the way that we see them. He looks at the heart. That night during prayer, God did show me my husband. But I was too blind to see the beauty that the Lord saw. It actually took a few years for the scales to be lifted from my eyes. But oh boy, when they were, WOW!

Another wedding took place shortly after. There were three weddings that I attended in two months. The second wedding that I went to, my future husband was there too. Again, I was in my own world. I could have had my husband time after time and it was my fault each moment the opportunity passed me by.

During this time I was attending a weekly Bible study. We were a group of six ladies and the subject was about shame. The study was to last for six weeks. When I started the lessons, I was feeling desperate for a husband as usual. This was the main issue that I worked on in my personal life. Then towards the middle of the Bible study, God changed me. I was left feeling that I didn't even want a husband anymore because it was so confusing and hurtful. I just didn't want to think that I found my husband only to be disappointed again. Every time that I met a man in church I was asking myself and God, "is he the one?" So as the Bible study and the weeks went on I finally came to the point in my life that I was happy with myself and God. I didn't feel as desperate for a husband as I did before. I didn't feel as though I should give up on the idea of having a husband either. I finally felt that it's okay. What, when, and who God wants for me will be perfect.

Of course I would continue to pray for God to send my husband to me. But now it was different. I became less self centered. I thought of my future husband having the same pain and struggles as I did. Then I became sad for him. I made it my mission to pray for him. Not for him to come into my life, but really pray for him. All of the energy that I had wasted on selfish prayers I turned it into positive prayer for my husband. I prayed for God to ease his pain, loneliness, and hurts. Every time that I would feel lonely, I turned it around and prayed for him. Every time that I felt angry, I prayed for him. Whatever I would feel about being without him, I used it as a weapon of prayer. I expressed my love for him through prayer even before I met him.

Sometime during the middle of December our church hosted a singles retreat. The man of God that was speaking was right on. He said that as he prayed and sought the Lord about what he should say to us, the Lord told him that His people were angry. Oh, how true that was for me!

My mother had died in the beginning of that same year and I was desperately longing for a husband. I knew that God was in control of both of those issues. I thought, *Who am I, that I could have the audacity to be angry with God?* Because I thought that way, I held it all inside. I tried to hide it from myself and God. But I was very angry and I didn't want to admit it or deal with it. But that weekend I did. I had to learn that it was alright to be angry.

I learned that anger is a God-given emotion. It is actually a signal to us that there is something wrong. It's like when we have pain. The pain is a warning that there is something wrong in our body. Well, that is what anger is. There was definitely something not right with me. I held on to the anger for so long that it turned into bitterness and resentment.

What we do with our anger is so important. Once I allowed myself to feel the anger that I had towards God, I was able to deal with it and He was able to deliver me from it.

At the end of the weekend, the evangelist said to me that he and his wife would make special effort to pray for me. He also said that my blessing was on the way.

Less than two weeks passed and it was time for the third wedding. This particular wedding was in the same house as the first one. The house belonged to the couple whose wedding was the first of the three weddings. This wedding was supposed to have no guests. About two weeks before, it was decided that a few choice friends would be invited. I was one. I was so happy about this wedding. I wasn't thinking about myself at all. The Lord had blessed me with a very nice Christmas bonus and I was so excited to bless this couple with a substantial gift. As the wedding was about to start, I noticed when Troy walked in. I remember thinking to myself that he must be someone really special to my friends because only a few people were invited.

When the ceremony was over, Troy and I began talking. We sat together and talked the whole night. I remember at one point, someone took a picture of us. I have it now. What a treasure! At the end of the night, he helped me to gather my things. Because it was such a small and intimate gathering, most of the guests brought some type of food. It was a "potluck wedding." He helped me to wash and dry some bowls that I brought.

Then he walked me out. As he helped me to put my things into my truck, I noticed that I forgot to take something out of my truck and it was still on the floorboard. Someone that I worked with had given me a few bottles of non-alcoholic sparkling juice. She knew that I didn't drink and thought that I would like to have them. I wanted to be nice and I thought that I would just toss it out later. The only thing was I forgot them in there. Well, when I opened my door for Troy to put my things in, he saw them. I quickly grabbed them and held them up in each hand and shouted out that I don't drink! We both continuously laughed even as I tried to explain what they were.

I was expecting him to ask me out or ask for my phone number or something to let me know that he was interested in me. During our conversation earlier in the night I mentioned to him that I had a dog, and I was looking for another home for it. What a coincidence, he was interested in finding a dog for his mother because she had recently lost hers. He wanted to give me his phone number and I told him no, I would give him mine. I said that I would not call a man. At this point, I was determined that I was not going to chase any man. So I gave him my number, then I shook his hand. That's right, I shook his hand. It was a nice firm handshake too. I showed him that I was a strong and independent woman.

After many years of waiting, praying and crying out to God, my dreams finally came true! God brought Troy into my life, only by this time I was afraid to believe it. In a way, he has been there from a distance for a while. He was able to see Tyler grow up from a toddler.

You may know some people in church that have unofficial parking places and seats. Once we find something that we are comfortable with we don't like to change. We are creatures of habit. I worked late every weekday and our midweek service started at 7:00 p.m. I didn't have much time to pick up my son from day care and feed us a decent meal. So we formed a routine. After picking him up, we would go to a drive-thru that was close to the church, grab some burgers and sit in the church parking lot to eat our dinner. It turned out that Troy's unofficial parking spot was right in front of mine. I remember him often pulling up in front of us and giving a small wave, usually right as I was taking a big bite of my burger. I would give him a tiny crooked smile with a mouth full and think to myself, *Oh here is that guy again catching me with my mouth full.* It happened every Wednesday.

Another time, after church, he was sitting on the camera stand and I walked over to some of my friends and he jumped down and almost ran over to me to introduce himself. This was very Holy Ghost inspired. Anyone who knew Troy would never imagine him being so forward. It simply is not his character. He never promotes himself. I was just standing there amazed at this man coming over so quickly to meet me. I didn't really think much about him as a prospective husband at that time. The Lord knew that I had a long way to go. It was about three and a half years worth of a long path.

Why Me, O Lord?

It was December 29th when we officially met at the wedding. That night was the first time in all of those years of seeing each other here and there at church; that we actually sat and talked together. It really is funny that he was there the whole time. I am grateful to God for that because Troy was able to see Tyler as a baby and a toddler.

God is a right-on-time kind of God! Troy felt during prayer that the Lord would bless him with "the one" in that year. By the time that this third wedding finally took place he was very disappointed because he thought that maybe he missed God's voice. There was only two days left to the year.

So after I gave him my number that night, I waited. I was very excited because I did like him. I just wanted to be very careful to not become too eager. I just couldn't go through the disappointment of being wrong again. The next day came and went with no phone call. The day after that one we had a New Year's Eve church service and I mentioned to a friend that I met him. I told her that I was excited and waiting for him to call, but only as a friend. She asked me if I felt that excited when I was waiting for my "girl" friends to call. Of course, I said no.

He did call that day after church and it was New Year's Eve and we told each other about our plans. I was hoping that he would catch my hint and show up, but he didn't. I believe that he called me the next day and from then on we started talking on a regular basis. The following weekend he was coming to see if my dog was the one that he wanted for his mom.

He came to my house to see the dog and I was painting Tyler's room. My dad was there visiting me and we had plans to go to visit my grandmother later that day. I told my dad that Troy would not be there long because he was just coming to see the dog. When he got out of the car and walked over to me, I was amazed. It was like it was the first time that I had seen him. The scales fell from my eyes and I saw him in a whole new light. He was very handsome. I loved his new haircut and the jeans! Oh, the jeans looked great on him.

You must understand; I was not very attracted to the way he liked to dress up in fancy suits. I didn't really like that too much. Not because I dress up nicely or even care about fashion, because I don't really. That was the problem. I liked jeans and a tee-shirt. The only time that I would really see him was at church or at weddings. He was always dressed up.

Now that day, when I saw him, he was beautiful to me. We talked for hours! He didn't really care about the dog. He really liked me. Even better than that, I really liked him too! Oh, thank You God! He was the one that I have waited for! There was only one problem. I was very scared to let myself enjoy what was happening because I just didn't want to be wrong again.

There I was, telling everyone I knew that I met this man. But I would also say that he wasn't the one. I told my family, friends and my very best friend. It wasn't until I said that to her that I realized what I was doing. She said to me "Oh hush up, you know that he is the one." From that moment on, I knew that she was right. I had finally been found by the one that I was looking for.

Chapter 10
Grow Where You Are Planted

Chapter 10

Grow Where You Are Planted

About six months after Troy and I were together, I knew that I had to leave the church that I loved so dearly. Although we met at White Dove, Troy had started going to a different church. Because his mother didn't drive, he took her to church after his father died. He went with her for moral support and slowly became a member of that church. The pastor there saw a calling on Troy's life for the ministry and he wanted to personally raise him up and train him for that purpose.

I knew that in order to be under God's authority, I had to go there. I refused to leave White Dove without getting a blessing from my pastor, so we scheduled an appointment. I will never forget how nervous Troy and I both were. We went into his office and sat down. Pastor didn't say anything for a minute and we just looked at him waiting for him to speak. When he did, he turned to Troy, looked him in the eyes and calmly said to him "I'm going to kill you." Then we all started laughing. He said that he was only going to let me go on a loan. He said that we would be back. He knew in the Spirit that he had to let us go and that we would return to him.

He gave us his blessing and said that he would be honored to co-officiate our wedding with the other pastor.

Why Me, O Lord?

Then I was released to Troy and to the other church. I loved my pastor and my church family. It was like multiple deaths to me. It was one of the hardest things that I ever had to go through. Yes, I had been abused and raped and even lost my mother. I had gone through a great deal of stuff in my life. But nothing that I had ever gone through compared to the pain that I felt at that time. This was different because it was a spiritual grieving.

I have to say that there was nothing wrong with the other church. It was a great church with wonderful pastors. What I am talking about is my perception of the way that things were for me. I can't stress enough that the other church was good to us. They recognized a calling on my husband's life and nurtured it. They gave us training and experience that we really needed. It was just really hard for me to make the transition from one church to another. It is beyond me how people can switch churches like they change their clothes. It was a family experience that I had never known before.

I was in culture shock. I began grieving the loss of my friends and church family at White Dove. I knew that I was ready to go. I knew that God had told me that it was time to move on. I knew that Troy was meant to be my husband. I knew all of these things, but it hurt so terribly. I finally had everything that I was waiting for. I had the man of my dreams and we were going to get married. There was only one problem. I was not prepared for the pain and grief of leaving White Dove. *Why me, O Lord?*

I dove into a deep depression, again. I began to get angry with and resent Troy's mother. I blamed her for me being away from my church. She just kept on trying to love me, but I didn't make it easy.

I began to wonder if I was supposed to even be with Troy. I knew what the Lord had told me. I knew that he was to be my husband and I also knew that I was supposed to be at his church. All of this was so hard for me. Then I began to be tormented by demons. Sitting next to Troy in church, I would feel the oppression of the devil. It was as though he was along side of me breathing on and screaming at me. I felt so much darkness. I was so tempted to just take off my ring and put it on the seat next to Troy and just run out of there, but I had enough grace from God to fight it.

As time went on, I fought hard to keep my relationship with Troy. I knew what the Lord had promised me and I was going to have it. Remember that you have to fight to be blessed! The devil doesn't want God to be glorified. He will fight you to try to make you give up on the blessing before you get it. I refused to let the devil steal him away from me. I worked to have a relationship with Troy's family and also with everyone in church.

We decided to go to pre-marriage counseling. We went to a wonderful Christian woman that didn't know either one of us. She helped us to be as ready for marriage as two people could be. I would recommend to anyone to make pre-marriage counseling a priority above all other wedding expenses. It was truly more beneficial to us than the dress, limousines, flowers, food, pictures, video or anything else.

We finally made it to the altar. Both of our pastors performed the ceremony. It was beautiful. Everything was going great until it came time for a reading of scripture. At that point a baby started screaming and the mother didn't take the child out. At that moment, to me, the screams of the baby represented the many devils that tried to break up Troy and I. They were defeated.

Why Me, O Lord?

From that day until now, I can count on one hand the number of major fights or arguments that we have had. My pastor said to the entire congregation that he believed that this was a good, good, move of the Holy Ghost. He told everyone that Troy couldn't do what God has called him to do without me by his side. He also said that Troy and I were only on loan to the other pastors. He said that we would be back. We belonged to him. I held that close to my heart.

As we said our vows to each other, we quoted scripture from the book of Ruth. "Your people will be my people, and your God will be my God." With this I decided that I would take his family as my own as well as his church family. From that moment on, I really worked hard to do the best that I could to be at peace with everyone. Troy and I didn't fight anymore. I began to love his mother and the rest of his family—church included. They all loved me so much. I just didn't really know how to receive all of that love.

I did better for a while, until the depression came back. I felt trapped. I started getting headaches when it was time for church so I wouldn't go. This became a regular thing. I was starving spiritually but not because the food wasn't prepared; I just didn't pick it up to eat it. I didn't realize that I basically went on a spiritual hunger strike when I left White Dove. Then one Sunday evening it was time for us to go and I said that I wasn't going. My husband said to me that he wasn't going to argue or plead with me. He simply said that he was very concerned about my relationship with the Lord. Then he left.

That was exactly what I needed for the Holy Ghost to minister to me. I laid in my bed and cried. I actually reminded myself of when I was a teen. Something then clicked in me and it was like a sudden transformation. I felt boldness come up from my belly and then I got out of bed and I stood by my window and looked outside. I cried out to God! I asked Him to make Himself real to me again. I had to put forth effort and with that, He did. He made Himself real to me again! I was in my own personal revival.

I decided that I was going to worship God with my all no matter where I was. I started to serve more in the church. I began doing nursery, greeting and the PowerPoint ministries. I made sure that the pastor and the singers had water before service began. I poured myself into everything that I could. I learned many small treasures during this time. I learned to grow where I was planted.

After I was at the new church for a while, I started to adjust and I formed relationships with others. Things were going very well for us. Troy and I decided to start trying for a baby. After only three months of trying, we were blessed! I was pregnant. The people of the church loved my baby long before he was even born. About six weeks before he was due, I told Troy that I was having pains every ten minutes. We were sitting in church at the time, so he wrote a note to our pastor and we tried to slip out. That is a hard thing to do when you are almost eight months pregnant and the entire family gets up from the front row in the middle of the pastor preaching. So he told everyone that I was going to the hospital and they all began to cheer. I didn't want them to cheer, I wanted them to pray. It was too soon!

Thankfully the doctors and nurses were able to calm the contractions and I went home. It was just a couple weeks later and Troy had an opportunity to preach a midweek service. It was fantastic. Later that night, the contractions started coming steady. I told Troy as calmly as I could, that

I needed him to take me to the hospital. I will never forget the look on his face. His eyes opened so wide. I think that he was still excited from preaching. I had never seen him look so scared before. I was a bit nervous too because, although it was a few weeks later, it was still too soon. I hoped that they could just stop the contractions like they did before. They told me to drink lots of water and walk around a lot, and they sent me home again.

The very next night, at about the same time, I woke Troy up and asked him to take me to the hospital again. Now the contractions were every five minutes. This time they couldn't stop them. I was already dilating and the baby was coming. They got me ready and by the time that my doctor came to do the exam; he said that we would have this baby within ten minutes. It was a very long night because by this time it was 8:00 a.m. the next day.

The doctor was right! My baby was born at 8:08 a.m. Troy was right there with me and witnessed the birth of our baby. I asked my doctor what was the sex of the baby. I frustrated everyone because I really wanted the surprise of waiting to know the gender. He had to flip him over to see and proudly announced, "It's a boy!" Then the nurse took the baby but I knew that something was wrong. My baby wasn't crying! I asked, "what was wrong, why didn't I hear the baby cry?" Then the nurse brought him over to me all wrapped up in the blanket and I held him. Only a few minutes passed and they took him to clean him and Troy went along so I started to rest.

A little while later, my husband and the nurse came in and I could tell that Troy was trying to tell me something, but he couldn't speak. Then the nurse stepped in and told me that there was a problem with Joshua. Because he didn't cry after birth, his lungs held fluid and he was unable to breathe enough oxygen. He had to be in the NICU. I was devastated! I couldn't have my baby with me.

I had to use the wheelchair to go to the NICU only to look at him through a window. I couldn't hold him or even touch him. Slowly he began making progress and Troy and I were allowed to go in to see him. Then as more time passed, we were able to hold him and I was thrilled!

The time came for me to be discharged from the hospital. Joshua was doing much better but he still was not ready to go. I cannot describe the pain that I had when I had to leave the hospital without my baby. No one expects to go into the hospital for such a joyous event as having a baby, only to leave without the baby. I was so grateful that he was alive and that in a few days he would be fine. But I was also so grieved that I was waiting in a wheelchair at the doors to head home... without my baby. *Why me, O Lord?*

I thank God that I had a very understanding and compassionate husband. We went to the hospital everyday to see our baby. My doctor wanted me to be at peace and take advantage of the time that I had to rest and recover. It was the longest three days of my life. Then the time finally came that he was to be discharged and come home!

Often times people will ask me questions when they find out that I am a Christian. They really have a question for God but they ask me. Someone once asked me how can a loving God allow children to die. How can anybody even begin to attempt answering such a question? I don't know. I honestly don't know. But this is what I do know. I know that God is good. He is not only good when everything in my life is wonderful, but He is good when things in my life are bad as well. He does not do things to hurt His children. He allows things to happen that will restore a relationship with them to Himself. I apologize, but this is my only answer that I have for such a question. God is good, all of the time. I trust Him.

III. Answered Prayers

Chapter 11

He Answers Prayers

Chapter 11

He Answers Prayers

As time went on, my husband grew greatly in the Lord. His preaching was stronger and with much revelation. Although he was being trained by this other pastor, he was nothing like him. It was amazing just how much he was like our first pastor. As he continued to grow, I supported him and poured myself into ministry—but I still missed White Dove.

He was asked to preach for a Wednesday service. Troy did such a great job in his preaching. Our pastor was in service and realized that he was no longer training to be a minister. He was a great preacher and teacher. Troy had served for years under this pastor but it was time to go a little farther in the ministry. We knew that the time had come for us to call our former pastor and ask for his advice.

Troy called him and had to leave a message asking him to return the call. He called back a few hours later and asked how I was. Troy said that I was fine, and then Pastor asked about the kids. Troy again said that they were fine. Pastor said, alright then the problem is you. Troy then talked to him about ministry. It was time for us to return to White Dove.

Why Me, O Lord?

We made an appointment with the pastor and his wife to explain that we were going back to our former pastor and that he would continue to raise us up and take us farther in the ministry. The pastor understood completely. After we talked everything out, we asked for his blessing. He suggested that we return one more Sunday so that we could also be blessed by the congregation. That is what we did. I am so glad that we did this. He was able to explain to everyone that God was moving us. After he did that the entire church blessed us. It was sort of like a receiving line at a wedding. Everyone came up to us and hugged us and told us goodbye. It was beautiful.

God was good to me. I could have taken what was given to me and become bitter about it, but I didn't. I became better because of it. Once I made the decision to make the best of my circumstances, and God's timing had arrived, He was able to move in our lives. I was obedient to God and supportive of my husband. I did not use any manipulation on Troy to try to get us to go back. I submitted to him and to God. God heard my cry. Finally, I was going home. We were going back to White Dove.

Often I wonder how it can be that God uses me. He chose me. Why? What can I do for Him? I guess that I can start by telling others what He has done for me. He saved me. He has promised eternal life (John 3:16). He loves me. He made me. He called me to be His very own. I have an inheritance. I am the righteousness of God in Christ Jesus. I am more than a conqueror and no weapon formed against me shall prosper (Isa. 54:17). I am above and not beneath. I am the head and not the tail (Duet. 28:13). I can do all things through Christ (Phil. 4:13). He wants to use me in ministry. Wait, what? He wants to use me in ministry? But I find myself asking, *Why me, O Lord?*

He has answered my every prayer. When I ⟨
He saved my life. When I dropped out of school, I
my father to take custody of me and put me back ⟨ school.
When I was single and pregnant, He took care of me. He is a
father to the fatherless and a husband to the husbandless.
I asked him to give me a son if I was going to be alone with
the baby, and He did. I asked Him for a house and He made
that happen. I asked for a new truck and I got one. He is
my Provider. I begged and pleaded for a husband and He
answered me. He said to wait for a while. But eventually,
He gave me His best.

Sometimes it takes a while for me to receive my answer,
but He always comes through. When my mom was diagnosed
with cancer, I started praying for her to be healed. He did
heal her, just not the way that I wanted Him to. And after
many years of praying for a husband, He gave me Troy.
After years of being away, He called us back to White Dove.
God blessed us abundantly in several different ways.

He even cares about the small things. I believe that He
answers silly prayers just to build our faith or sometimes just
because He wants to laugh. He wants us to talk with Him.

He wants what is best for us always. We must keep in
mind that He knows what He has in the future for us. He
wants to bless us. How often do we forget that He made
us? Would not God, who created us for His purpose, do
wonderful and mighty things for us? Not because we are
good, but because He is good.

I have realized that when something terrible happens to
me, yes, maybe the devil did it. But if the devil did it, then
God allowed it. If God allowed it, then it has to be for my
good. Maybe He will show me why He allowed it, or maybe
not. No matter what He decides, I will trust Him.

Why Me, O Lord?

God does answer all of our prayers. We just have problems receiving His answers. Sometimes we don't like the answer He gives. "Wait," "No," or even "Not the way you expect Me to." These are some of the answers that God gives. God's ways are not the same as our ways.

How many of us use logic instead of just trusting the Spirit? It doesn't matter what we are going through. God will always do what He knows is best for us. We may not understand His answers or we may think that He is telling us no when He may only be saying wait. Sometimes we may take a good idea and try to sign God's name on it only to get angry with God when it seems that He is not answering our prayers. Later we find out that His *not* answering was actually Him answering our prayers by not doing what we asked. We don't see the bigger picture the way God sees it. My pastors have taught us to pray for God to bless or block whatever it is that we may be praying for. That is especially effective when we are not quite sure of God's will on a certain issue. We must trust that He answers our prayers.

I have been through some stuff. I was used and abused. I was raped. I was an alcoholic and I was on drugs. I was in sexual sin. I was deeply depressed and I was suicidal. I was a single mother and I lost my mother. That is some of the stuff that I have been through. But now, I am on the other side. Now I am happy. I live in a beautiful house with a wonderful family. I am saved! I am truly blessed. I've gone through and I kept going. He kept me going. He has a reason and a purpose that He allowed all of those things for me to go through. I will use everything that I have gone through for His glory as He allows me to. He was there and He answered my prayers.

Chapter 12
The Storms
of Life

Chapter 12

The Storms of Life

Growing up in south Louisiana, everyone knew that they should keep an axe in their attics to be prepared for rising waters. Our grandparents told their children and our parents told us. Now we evacuate. That's what I did several times before. Pack a few days worth of clothes and try to find a hotel in a nice area where there will be lots of things to do to help pass the time. So what was one more time?

We left in the beginning of the voluntary evacuation. We were caught in evacuation traffic a year before for 19 hours so we didn't want to wait too long before getting on the road this time. Several hours later we arrived in Houston and were able to rent a room for at least one night. They would let us stay longer if someone canceled a reservation. Thankfully that did happen. That is where we witnessed on television the people who could not evacuate, standing in line to enter the Super Dome to be their shelter during the storm. At that time no one knew what to expect from hurricane Katrina.

After a few days we learned that we would not be allowed to return to our homes for quite some time. We found thrift stores to get a few more pieces of clothes and there were some people there that overheard us talking and they wanted to pay for our things. Now if it were the other way around, Troy and I would have done the exact same thing. This time was different. We were on the receiving end. The blessings started coming. We went to eat and the people at the table next to us paid our bill without us knowing. Time after time, God provided for us in similar ways. We were overwhelmed by the goodness of God through strangers.

We ended up staying in that same hotel room for six nights and we still didn't have any idea of when we would be allowed to return to our home. Tyler was with his father because when he left on Friday to spend the weekend with him, the storm was going to Florida, not New Orleans. My father and his wife invited us to stay with them for a while. I was still trying to locate anyone from my company and Troy was trying to find out the condition of his real estate rental property. All cell phones were out and there were no working land lines, not that there would have been anyone around to answer if there were working phones.

After a few more days I went to the public library near my father's house to use the internet and I finally found a contact with my company. The good news was that I still had a job. The bad news was that it was temporarily relocated to Lafayette, LA. That was a three hour drive from home. We left my dad's place for a hotel room that my company had reserved in Lafayette. By this time, we had met up with Tyler's father to get him back. So there we were, the four of us, in a hotel room still not knowing when we could return home.

When the authorities finally did open the roads to allow people to come back, it was only to evaluate the damages.

Troy went to check on our home and our rental properties. At home we needed a new roof and a new fence. That was great. The rental property, however, was hit by a tornado. There were a few tenants that stayed there to ride out the storm. They could not afford to evacuate and they didn't go to a shelter. They were okay. The tornado lifted the roof off of the corner apartment and left the roof on the apartments that they were in. Troy actually had to use his key to enter apartment 12, but once he did, he looked up and saw the sky. How was he going to fix this? He was a small business owner with a handful of apartments.

As he was trying to make sense of all the mess everywhere in one of his darkest hours, he noticed in the middle of all the trash and debris, a small bookmark. It said, "For where two or three gather together as my followers, I am there among them..." He looked up and saw the two guys that went with him and he knew that God also was with him.

My boss did provide housing for me. I had Troy's mom and my baby with me in Lafayette. Troy couldn't really be with me because he had to take care of the house and the apartments and Tyler's school re-opened. So I traveled back and forth to Lafayette. As I was getting ready for work in the morning, I noticed that my pastor was on one of the local Lafayette channels. I was so happy that I was able to have his ministry feeding me in such a difficult time. While I was there, I often prayed for God to make a way for Pastor Mike to have a White Dove church in Lafayette, LA.

Once Troy did restore the apartments, and we didn't collect any rent for the month following the storm, the demands of the apartments wore on Troy. I mentioned to him that it might be a good time to try to sell. Minutes later, he mentioned that idea to someone and immediately they said that they would buy them. With that, God blessed us tremendously. We were able to buy less demanding rental property as well as pay off our house. We went from not knowing if I had a job or if we had any apartments to being completely debt free!

It was five months after Katrina that my company was able to return to New Orleans. In December of 2005 my husband moved me back home and said in his heart that he would never return to Lafayette. We had no idea that God had different plans for us.

A few months later, Pastor Mike announced that he was going to plant a church in Lafayette. Troy and I both felt like we were punched in the gut when he made that announcement. We knew that we were called to be a part of it. We were blessed with the opportunity to help our pastor minister in a city that was a refuge to us. That was quite an honor for us to which we will always be grateful.

Hurricane Katrina was one of many storms of my life. Some storms cause devastation. Some bring a cleansing when they arrive. Storm clouds have silver linings and rainbows. It's extremely hard to imagine as we go through storms that just on the other side is a blessing. How do you handle the storms in your life? Do you give in to the devastation? Do you give up and not even look for the rainbow or the silver lining? Or, do you call out to God and ask Him to have His way with you and give you strength to endure as you go through? One thing that I know is that every storm will come to an end.

With hurricane Katrina, so many people were completely devastated. It was all over the news. There were deaths and rapes. Total and complete destruction was all around. My grandmother was one who lost everything. My aunt and uncle also lost everything. People that I worked with lost everything that they owned. I on the other hand, was blessed through the storm. To that I say... *Why me, O Lord?*

Chapter 13

What Did He See?

Chapter 13

What Did He See?

Something wonderful happened one Saturday afternoon. It was actually quite amazing in how everything lined up to create this divine appointment. Only weeks had passed since Troy and I had finished working on an outreach with our pastors. We used to travel every Saturday for a few years. But we were now free on Saturdays. I needed something that only one store in my area carried and it was across town, about an hour away. Usually my husband would get it for me during the week but he was unable to and we both decided to go.

We were going to do a few things in that area because we don't go there very often, but we ended up just going to get what I needed. While in the store after getting my things I wanted to look at the desserts. "I promise I was just looking at them and that was good enough to put on weight" I was joking with Troy. We were smiling and playing around and I looked over to see a man that was staring at me.

Suddenly my face drained of all my joy and my jaw dropped with awe. My eyes got big and my eyebrows rose in wonder. *Was it really him? After all of these years, can I be sure that it was really him?* He looked so much older and very fragile. We began walking toward each other. Troy realized that I knew the man, but he wasn't familiar to him. He thought that I must know him from work. If you could imagine a slow motion segment in a movie; that is exactly how this moment felt to me.

We slowly came together and I grabbed his hand with both of mine and held it and he said his name. Then I said my name, basically confirming that we were exactly who we thought each other was. Strangely, when I said my name I abruptly stopped after my first name. In about a tenth of a second the thought ran though my mind that my first instinct was to say my current last name, but he doesn't know me by that name. He only knew my maiden name, but I didn't identify myself with that name. That person seems so foreign to me now. It all happened so fast even though it felt long.

He said to me, "You look good." My eyes filled with tears as I stared him in the eyes. Then I introduced him to my husband and my youngest son, who was also with us. Troy then realized that this man was someone much more important to me than someone that I knew from work. I said to him "Thank you for everything that you did for me. Thank you." He just repeated himself. "You look good; you look so good." Then we walked away from each other.

I then explained to Troy who that man was. He was my doctor. He was the good doctor from my teenage years when I was in the psychiatric hospital. I believe that everyone has that special person, a mentor, that if they had not been in their lives, it all would have been different. To some it may be a pastor or a teacher. To others it may be a special aunt or a best friend. Well, this man was that to me. He helped me to want to live.

The entire day I was in awe. I constantly prayed asking God to show me what that divine appointment was for. Troy suggested that maybe it was for my doctor to see that what he did in his lifetime mattered. He made a difference. That is a nice thought. That after all of these years, I could be some sort of inspiration to him. But that still was not quite the answer that I was looking for.

I kept asking myself, Troy, everyone around me, and God, "What did he see?" What did my doctor see when he looked at me more than twenty years after me being his patient? Then it came to me. The words that he spoke to my father on the day that he finally discharged me from the hospital. "I was given a mess, but I give back to you, a ballerina princess."

That's it! That is what he saw when he looked at me. He did see a princess. I am a child of The King! He saw the light of the Lord. He saw a new creation. He saw a miracle. He saw God's glory.

Even as we forget the former things and press on, sometimes it is good to look back to see just how far we have come. I have learned in my journey to find answers that through all of my trials, testing, prayers, and questions, it never was about me. I found my answers in Him. It was always about Him. It was all about bringing glory to The Father.

A Special Note from the Author

Have you ever asked, *Why me, O Lord?* I'm sure that you have. We all have.

When you look at yourself in the mirror, what do you see? Do you see a child of God who is abundantly loved? Do you see someone that your parents are proud of? Do you see a successful life? Do you see a great future?

Maybe you see someone that you don't even recognize. Could it be someone that you don't even like or worse still, someone that you hate? When you looked at yourself in the mirror have you ever seen someone that you wanted to kill?

It was God's grace and the love of Jesus Christ that saved me. It doesn't matter who you are, where you are, or even how old you are. God made you for His purpose. He loves you. Next time you do find yourself asking, *Why me, O Lord?* ask yourself this question: Why *not* me? Do you have any idea just who you are?

- He created you to be His child in John 1:12.

- You are His friend in John 15:15.

- You are justified in Romans 5:1.

- You are a member of His body in 1 Corinthians 12:27.

Why Me, O Lord?

- You have been bought with a high price and you belong to God in 1 Corinthians 6:20.

- You are united with the Lord in 1 Corinthians 6:17.

- You have been redeemed and forgiven of all sins in Colossians 1:14.

- You are free from condemnation in Romans 8:1-2.

- You know that all things work together for good in Romans 8:28.

- You are certain that God, who began the good work within you, will continue His work until it is finally finished in Philippians 1:6.

- You are God's temple in 1 Corinthians 3:16.

Aren't you? Is Jesus your Savior? All you have to do is turn away from sin and ask Him to be. You don't have to go through life asking, *Why me, O Lord?* All of the answers are found in the Lord!

About the Author

So many years I have dealt with depression and suicidal thoughts. I almost died at my own hand at the age of fourteen. I was lost, lonely and desperate. I had no idea of the plans that God had for my life.

Today I am a very happy and blessed person. I have such a wonderful husband and two fantastic boys. I am blessed to be a member of White Dove Fellowship International Outreach Center in New Orleans, LA under the teachings and leadership of Pastor's Mike and Elaine Millé. I am also a licensed member of the Great Commission Fellowship.

To contact me please send an e-mail to:

melissacalegan@yahoo.com

More Titles by 5 Fold Media

Treasures of God
by Jane Cochran
ISBN: 978-0-9827980-4-1
$15.00

This is the story of the life of Jane Cochran; an ordinary woman, with an extraordinary God. Here you will find her account of how everyday issues and problems that she faced were turned upside-down when God stepped into the picture. Jane shares how angels have saved her many times from life-threatening situations.

As we go through trials, there will always be treasures...we just need to look for them.

Daddy, If You Only Knew
by Steve & Lennette Deal
ISBN: 978-0-9825775-0-9
$15.00

America has vastly become a fatherless nation. Now the children's voices uncut, unedited,and sometimes harsh are revealed regarding their relationships, or lack thereof, with their fathers. This book compiles some of their letters pouring out their hearts to their fathers, known and unknown.

"You will experience, from the pens of these children, their pain and the longing to be loved, nurtured, and taught by their Father."
- Abraham Brown,
Founder, Owner, Abe Brown Ministries

Visit www.5foldmedia.com to sign up for **5 Fold Media's FREE email update.** You will get notices of our new releases, sales, and special events such as book signings and media conferences.

A Word From the Publisher

Thank you so much for taking the time to read one of our books. I hope you enjoyed it! There is something else I would like you to read, and it will only take a moment of your time. You see, I am alive today because Jesus changed my life!

By the time I was two years old, I was given only six months to live due to a life-threatening blood disorder. It was at this time that my parents took me for prayer at their home church, calling on the name of the Lord. Shortly after this prayer, God intervened, and I was divinely healed just two weeks later. Jesus changed my life!

One afternoon in 1992, just three weeks before my high school graduation, I died of a drug overdose. This one event caused me to see Jesus face-to-face and also witness my dead, lifeless body down on earth. Through this incredible encounter I was brought back to life and instantly set free from drugs. Several weeks later, I gave my heart to the Lord in a county jail cell late on a Friday night. It was there that God called me by name and set me free from alcohol. Within one year, God sent me to Bible college where I met my wonderful wife, Cathy.

In my freshman year of college I was placed in remedial English due to my lack of skill in reading and writing. I certainly was not college material back then, but once again God had special plans. In 1999 I had another encounter with God that lasted nearly two and a half hours. This is when the Lord imparted to me the ability to prophesy and gave me the anointing to write. This is when the passion for creative media all began.

In the year 2000, I got involved with publishing, often working late evening hours to volunteer with media efforts behind the scenes. In 2005 I started writing a small, encouraging e-mail to five people each week. (I think two or three of them did not even care to read them!) This small beginning was discouraging, but God told me to keep on writing. I began writing on an international scale in 2008 and have continued to do so. Depending on what venues take these writings God gives me, they are sent to well over three hundred thousand potential viewers worldwide.

Not only did the Lord implant in me a desire to prophesy and write, He also put within me a longing for knowledge. After earning a bachelor of arts degree in Bible from Central Bible College in Springfield, Missouri, I continued my studies at Freedom Seminary in Rogers, Arkansas. There I received my master's degree and doctorate in Christian education, earning the status of summa cum laude and President's honor roll. Once again, Jesus changed my life!

These are some of the many reasons 5 Fold Media, LLC was founded. We are passionate about creative media and seeing lives changed for Jesus. God broke my addictions and then took my inability to write and turned it into a promising opportunity to touch the world for Him. God has changed my life!

God bless,
Dr. Andy Sanders
Publisher, 5 Fold Media, LLC

5 Fold Media, LLC is a Christ-centered media company. Our desire is to produce lasting fruit in writing, music, art, and creative gifts.

"To Establish and Reveal"
For more information visit:
www.5foldmedia.com

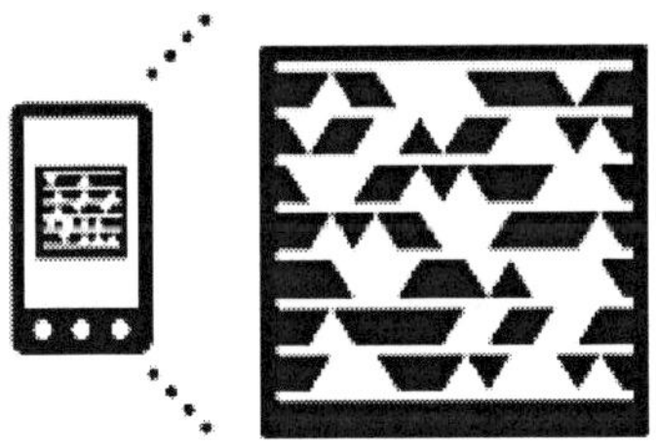

Use your mobile device to scan the tag above and visit our website. Get the free app: http://gettag.mobi